Arabella

PALMETTO
PUBLISHING
Charleston, SC
www.PalmettoPublishing.com

Copyright © 2024 by Allie Hardwick

All rights reserved
No portion of this book may be reproduced, stored in a retrieval system, or transmitted in any form by any means-electronic, mechanical, photocopy, recording, or other-except for brief quotations in printed reviews, without prior permission of the author.

Paperback ISBN: 9798822959989

Arabella
The most exceptional one-eyed cat in Georgia

Allie Hardwick

Illustrated by Silas Koyama. Photographs by Belinda Jeffries

To all, with or without children, who have loved their cats, I dedicate this book.

We moved from Washington D.C. to Atlanta, Georgia in 1989. And in the process of moving in I became aware of a daily occurrence happening on my street. Around 4 o'clock each afternoon three adolescent grey cats were met by a wad of white fur whom I took to be their mommy. They rubbed noses to greet each other and then proceeded to their home across the street. I began to look forward each day to this gathering.

And then one lovely day the white wad appeared at our screened porch. "Well," said I. The white wad was indeed a fluff ball of a cat with a wounded eye who looked at me plaintively. "What?" said I. It seemed she wanted in. So, I opened the screen door, and she began to look the place over carefully and then apparently decided our porch would do, lay down and went to sleep. When she wanted out I heard about it even in the back of the house.

What I thought was a one-time event began to happen every day. So, in order to keep my life simple, we put in a cat door, created a comfy sleeping box, and named the cat Arabella. There was no hesitation over the naming. She was a big time Arabella. And in due time she let me know she wanted to explore the house. Again, I opened a door and in she went. She picked her sleeping spot and settled in, usually staying put until four when she was due for high tea on Harold avenue (I could see it was a very formal event) to greet her boys.

Of course we began assuming the cat was really ours. After all, she chose us. But our notion was disturbed when we heard our neighbor was moving to Arizona. She had two huge dogs, the three boys, and Arabella.

I went immediately and urgently across the street to inquire about Arabella. To my immense relief my neighbor said that she was worried about how Arabella would make the move and she could be ours with one request. Would we please keep her name. "What is that", I inquired. "Chloe," she said. So, Arabella became on that day Chloe Arabella, though never in a million years could this cat be a Chloe. Then she told me Arabella's history

Our neighbor was a director at one of Atlanta's live theaters and she, while at work, became aware of the constant presence of this white cat who hung out in the back alley and was often found asleep on the trash cans. She had a wounded eye and our neighbor in a fit of compassion took her to the vet. The vet gave her all her shots, cleaned her up and pronounced the eye beyond help. Our neighbor adopted her on the spot and took her home. This explained to me why Arabella did not want a soft place on which to sleep. In fact, this explained why, when our daughter came for a visit and brought her cat and kitty litter, Arabella, who had never seen kitty litter, decided this was a great place to sleep. Instant education followed. We have a wonderful picture of her sleeping on a encyclopedia.

But a time came when my husband, who is a university professor and an Episcopal priest, decided he wanted to be a full-time priest and accepted a position in Washington, Georgia, the deep South. I am a Texan, as is my husband, so I did not know a thing about the deep South. My husband was better acclimated because his formative years were in Memphis, Tennessee, and Meridian, Mississippi. We, along with our neighbor, wondered how Arabella would take the move, not to mention how I would take the move.

So let me tell you about Washington, Georgia. It was not your typical small town.

From February 1781 to 1782 Washington was the capital of Georgia, but the railroad went through Atlanta and the capital ended up there. A revolutionary battle was fought just outside Washington. But Washington figured most prominently in the Civil War. Robert Toombs, who was the Confederate Secretary of State for six months, had a fine house next to the Episcopal church.

The Vice-President of the Confederacy lived a few miles south. There were twenty-nine properties listed on the National Historic Registry. One of those properties was the Mary Willis Library, which was built in 1888 and was the first free library in George. The main window in the library is a Tiffany created in memory of Mary Willis. But the library's main claim to fame was the Confederate treasure chest, which was brought from Richmond to Washington by Jefferson Davis where and when he dissolved the Confederacy. The library often has visitors looking for the Confederate gold. The chest was completely empty as was the Confederate treasury at the end of the war. The Episcopal Church of the Mediator has windows done by internationally known designer Wilbur Burnham who has stained glass windows in the National Cathedral in Washington D.C. Washington, Georgia is a swarm of antebellum houses. It is a hot bed of old South manners and traditions and an incredibly lovely town. This was where we were headed.

The movers came, the boxes proliferated, confusion reigned. Arabella coped. And I fretted about what lay ahead. I mean, Texans are frontier and not always couth and I was headed to Couthville. As an example of not being totally civilized, I never saw the point of setting the table just so. It made sense to me to put all eating implements on one side of the plate. Consequently, my children never had a chance to be mistaken for a groomed deep Southerner. Well, besides, their accents would be wrong.

But the van pulled away with all our possessions. The time had come to get on with it. We, with great care and concern, gave Arabella a tranquillizer. She rode in a slightly loopy state on the dashboard of the borrowed Eddie Bauer pick-up truck just ahead of the steering wheel. She definitely had a sense of place. And she was the center of everyone's attention when the truck stopped at a light.

We arrived and sat for a while to survey our new home, a vicarage. I felt oddly like a character in an Agatha Christie novel. Then we released Arabella trusting her to stick with us. The first thing she saw was an enormous domesticated black and white bunny rabbit. (I never saw the creature again.) Arabella's eyes were like pinwheels. Perhaps she thought she had arrived in wonderland. Boxes were unloaded by movers, and we, accompanied by Arabella, went in.

And thus began our life in a new place. (We discovered later that Arabella considered she had arrived at her true home.) The Episcopal church had done everything they could think of to make our entry into their lives as comfortable as possible. One lovely parishioner arrived that day with a 409 cleaner saying, no doubt, we would need this. And another arrived with Evelyn's chocolate cake. All of this reminded me of my life as a child. My father was a Methodist minister and each time we moved to a new church there would be a box of staples and other necessary items so we could get on with it. I thought we were a charity case. This was in the depression. And Daddy often got paid in chickens. What would I think at an age too young to understand the depression? Now I had to rethink the whole thing

So, we settled in and established routines in our lives. This would become Arabella's. She slept in, ate her breakfast, had a drink, and then headed to the Robert Toombs House. She obviously concluded that this was the most prestigious place in town and that she should be there. The house is on the National Historic Registry and is opened daily for tours. Arabella assumed she added to the historical era and I know if she had a hoop skirt, she would gladly have worn it. Missing the skirt, she sat daily on the front porch greeting visitors. The crew at the house apparently thought Arabella added an aura so she was welcomed. In fact, we got a call one day telling us that the porch at the house was being painted and they hoped this did not upset Arabella. She became a fixture there. Occasionally people were granted permission to have special events there and the staff had to explain that Arabella was part of the crew since she would sit at the windows looking plaintive and usually she was let in. In spite of the injured eye she was a beautiful cat, long haired, incredibly fluffy, and unashamedly regal. She outdid Scarlett O'Hara. Arabella soon had a reputation in town.

Meanwhile the rest of us were learning the town, meeting the people, and tending the church. Meanwhile, Arabella's soul was in its element. And the priest and I were enormously interested in the citizens of Washington, Georgia.

Then one day Arabella's realm expanded. The priest and I received an invitation to a grand dinner just down the street. We had no idea what to expect except we knew the house and that it had been lovingly restored by two natives of Atlanta, Robert and Robert. The house was indeed worth restoring. Two justices of the Supreme Court, father and son, had lived there. In fact, their two houses were combined. It was one of the wonderful ones with huge windows that could become doors, and which opened upon a veranda which went around three sides of the house. We were thrilled to have been invited. Since it was just down the street we walked. When we got to the house, we became aware that our two cats (we had acquired another), Daphne and Arabella, were right behind us. There was no shooing them away and taking them home would make us late to the gathering. Daphne situated herself in a parked convertible and Arabella followed us into the house. She was in heaven.

She greeted all the guests. She determined the kitchen was on the lower level and down she went where she was immediately fed pieces of ham. She returned upstairs where she sat on the piano where a person who would become a great friend, was playing. Arabella settled herself there. She was petted by one and all.

And eventually she went back to her duty of mingling with guests. Robert and Robert assumed she added a zing to their dinner and didn't seem to mind she was there. When it was time to leave, we figured we would try to lure the cats' home with us. We called and Daphne popped up out of the car and Arabella eventually appeared, grousing all the way home. We found out the next day that she went back to the party and stayed until all the guests went home and the Roberts turned out the lights.

  Somehow Arabella knew about the Historic Register. She was faithful in her duties at the Robert Toombs house and rarely deviated from her routine. However, through her internal network, she got word that an important gathering was happening at the Masonic Lodge (indeed on the Historic Register) and she attended to the amusement of all. There was no way to ignore her as she greeted everyone, then sat herself down in the first row. I am sure someone said, "How nice of you to join us". We heard about this after the fact. One day a parishioner reported that Arabella had visited their house. It apparently had the Arabella stamp of approval and all in the house were honored.

Arabella had her close calls. We returned home one night to frantic screams. An owl had Arabella in her grasp and Arabella had all 4 feet in motion. I think the screaming was coming from the owl who had to drop her. It was about a ten-foot drop and of course Arabella landed on her feet. We were very busy after that counting our cats. By this time we had more. Maybe Arabella had a network and posted that the food was good, and the house was warm. They appeared at our front door in a constant stream. Maybe there was a hidden cat hobo sign on the vicarage wall. Arabella did not seem to mind the additions to the family. After all, she spent her time at the Robert Toombs House. But one parishioner commented that surely we were the only church in town with fur hood ornaments.

And another time she was treed by two stray dogs, and I found her hanging on a branch with one hind leg dangling. Off to the vet. Arabella was enhanced with a huge bandage on her leg. This was very hard for her to bear. Her image was threatened. And after a few days she was bandage free. We could not find it and assumed she had eaten it off. Yuck!! The leg healed without it.

  A year went by, and another invitation came to the Roberts' lovely do. This time the priest and I crept away without cats. We arrived and a Robert asked us where Arabella was. Apparently she was included in the invitation. We went home and got her. She was thrilled and went about greeting all. At one point a Robert told me that one of their guests pointed out in a rather shocked voice that there was a cat under the buffet table eating shrimp. "That is Arabella", said Robert. "she is an invited guest." She closed this party down, too. We didn't even bother calling her home.

  And the next year we received the annual invitation with a drawing of a cat with an arrow, so we did not miss it. And the next year Arabella received the invitation with a note that told her she could bring us if she wanted to.

Arabella was the sort of cat one did not boss around. She was in charge of her life and we needed to keep remembering this. One lovely example of this was the time we went walking in the evening on Robert Toombs Avenue, the main street through town. Arabella, of course, accompanied us. When we elected to return home, we picked her up and carried her across the street accompanied with much whining. We put her down and she turned around, went back across the street, looked both ways, and returned. So there! She had to remind us again. We tried hard to keep this in mind. We knew she knew how to take care of herself. She had one wonderful trick to let us know that. When she did her daily cleaning, licking all human contact off her body and covering same with cat spit, she would crawl onto the priest, lick his beard, then rub her head vigorously on said beard. Brilliant! Every inch clean!

Oddly enough she did not often try to get in the church even though it was an historic site. She did, however, frequent the Presbyterian Church which was our neighbor. Apparently, the church members who prepared the church for Sunday services kept finding white hairs on the green upholstered pastor's chair, the best seat in the house. The church was carefully locked. This was a great mystery, and everybody suspected Arabella. A great search commenced. Finally someone found a basement vent through which she must have entered.

We never knew Arabella's age having not been present at her beginning. We lived seventeen years in Washington, four of which we were without her. She died of an awful cancer of the mouth. I could tell she felt humiliated with such an affliction. We chose to take her life and she died in the arms of the priest and myself. She took a portion of our hearts. We wrote an obituary and the paper published it without question. We dedicated the flowers on the alter to her. She is buried at the end of the church's parking lot, a blessed burial site for a bevy of beloved critters. We can honestly say that we do not expect to meet a cat with Arabella's soul again in our lifetime. She was a once in a lifetime event. But I can tell you that she lives vividly in the souls of the priest and I.

    We have since moved to Virginia, leaving Arabella in her true home.

About the Author:

Allie Hardwick is 87 years old and without a clue how she got there. One day she just was. She grew up with dogs but when she married the priest she was soon awash in cats. There was no doubting they were an interesting bunch. Arabella stood out. But to this day she is not sure Arabella was a cat. Allie lives in the Shenandoah Valley, an incredibly lovely part of the earth.

About the Illustrator:

Silas Koyama is a sophomore at the College of Wooster in Ohio. He has now taken to painting but was pressured into illustrating with line drawings, for which all are grateful. He was not lucky enough to know Arabella.

www.ingramcontent.com/pod-product-compliance
Lightning Source LLC
LaVergne TN
LVHW021953060526
838201LV00049B/1696